SAVE OUR ANIMALS!

Giant Panda

Louise and Richard Spilsbury

Heinemann
LIBRARY

www.heinemann.co.uk/library
Visit our website to find out more information about Heinemann Library books.

To order:
☎ Phone 44 (0) 1865 888066
▤ Send a fax to 44 (0) 1865 314091
▭ Visit the Heinemann Bookshop at www.heinemann.co.uk/library to browse our catalogue and order online.

First published in Great Britain by Heinemann Library, Halley Court, Jordan Hill, Oxford OX2 8EJ, part of Harcourt Education.
Heinemann is a registered trademark of Harcourt Education Ltd.

Editorial: Kate Bellamy, Diyan Leake, Cassie Mayer, and Katie Shepherd
Design: Michelle Lisseter and Ron Kamen
Illustrations: Bridge Creative Services
Cartographer: Vickie Taylor at International Mapping
Picture research: Hannah Taylor and Fiona Orbell
Production: Duncan Gilbert

Origination: Chroma Graphics (Overseas) Pte. Ltd.
Printed and bound in China by South China Printing Co. Ltd.

The paper used to print this book comes from sustainable resources.

10 digit ISBN 0 431 11426 9
13 digit ISBN 978 0 431 11426 2

10 09 08 07 06
10 9 8 7 6 5 4 3 2 1

British Library Cataloguing in Publication Data
Spilsbury, Louise and Richard
Save the giant panda. – (Save our animals!)
599.7' 89
A full catalogue record for this book is available from ...y.

Spilsbury, Loui

Giant panda /
Louise and
Richard

J599.
789

1685780

nts
...ould like to thank the following for
...produce photographs: Ardea pp. **4** top
... top left (J Rajput); Corbis pp. **22, 28** (K
... Brazil/ Stringer); Digital Vision pp. **5**
.../Minden Pictures p. **10** (K Wothe);
...ina Photos pp. **19, 23, 26, 29**;
.... **4** bottom, (M Carwardine), **17** (S
...**7** (A Bannister); Oxford Scientific pp. **4** middle, **5** top right, **13, 14, 27** (K Su);
Photolibrary.com/Oxford Scientific pp. **6, 12**; Still Pictures pp. **5** bottom, **9, 21** (F Polking), **15** (M Carwardine), **16** (Uniphoto Press), **18** (Zi Yi/UNEP); WWF p. **25**.

Cover photograph of giant panda, reproduced with permission of Corbis Sygma/ Bill Vaughn.

The publishers would like to thank staff at WWF Qinling Panda Focal Project for their assistance in the preparation of this book.

Every effort has been made to contact copyright holders of any material reproduced in this book. Any omissions will be rectified in subsequent printings if notice is given to the publishers.

Contents

Animals in trouble 4

The giant panda 6

Where can you find giant pandas? 8

What do giant pandas eat? 10

Young giant pandas 12

Natural dangers 14

Hunting and trapping 16

Dangers to the giant panda's world 18

How many giant pandas are there? 20

How are giant pandas being saved? 22

Who is helping giant pandas? 24

How can you help? 26

The future for giant pandas 28

Giant panda facts 30

More books to read 30

Glossary 31

Index 32

Some words are shown in bold, **like this**. You can find out what they mean by looking in the Glossary.

Animals in trouble

There are many different kinds, or **species**, of animal. Some species are in danger of becoming **extinct**. This means that all the animals from that species might die.

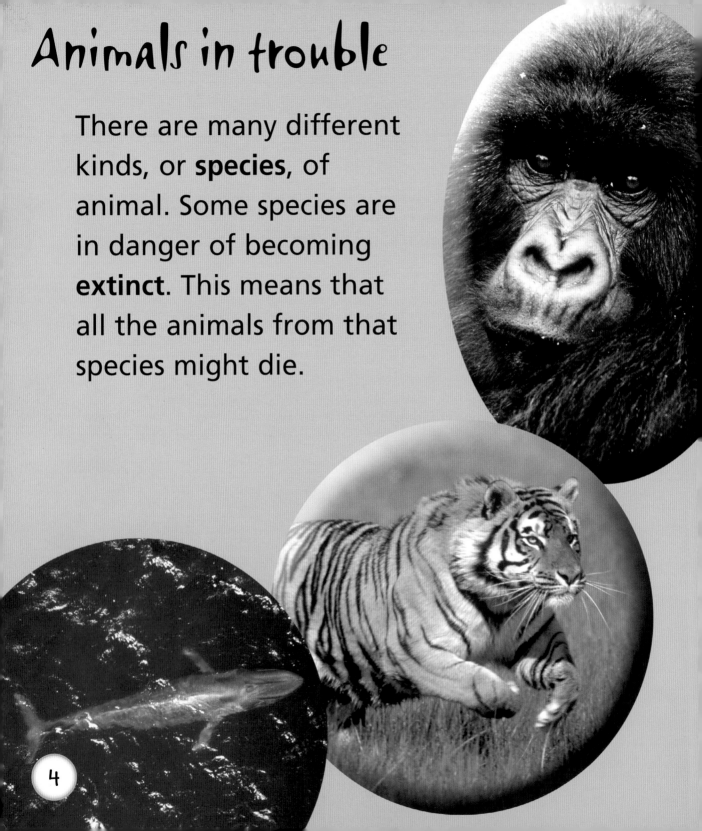

All the animals shown here are in danger of becoming extinct. These species need to be saved. The giant panda is one of them.

The giant panda

Giant pandas are very easy to recognize. They are large, fluffy bears with black and white hair. Their legs, shoulders, ears, and eye patches are black.

A giant panda has ovals of black hair around its eyes.

Pandas use their sharp claws to help them climb trees.

Giant pandas mainly stay on the ground and walk on their four legs. They may climb trees to sleep or to look around. They grip things with their claws.

Where can you find giant pandas?

In the past, giant pandas lived all over southern and eastern China. They also lived in Myanmar and Vietnam. Today they only live in a few parts of South-west China.

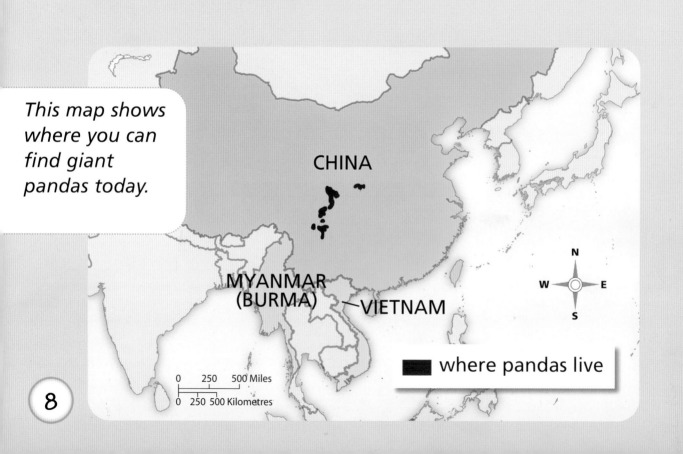

This map shows where you can find giant pandas today.

CHINA

MYANMAR
(BURMA)

VIETNAM

N
W — E
S

0   250   500 Miles
0   250 500 Kilometres

■ where pandas live

Giant pandas live on mountain slopes like these.

Giant pandas live in forests on high mountain slopes. It is cold and rainy there. The giant panda's thick, woolly hair keeps it warm and dry.

What do giant pandas eat?

Giant pandas only eat **bamboo**.
Bamboo is a kind of giant grass plant.
They eat the **shoots**, stems, and leaves
of bamboo plants.

The giant panda has five short fingers and a long wrist-bone.

Giant pandas have to eat a lot of bamboo to stay healthy. They can spend about 16 hours of every day eating.

Giant pandas usually sit down to eat. They hold food in their front paws.

Young giant pandas

Baby pandas are called **cubs**. They are usually born in a cave. They stay there for six weeks. Pandas are **mammals**, so the cubs drink milk from their mother.

This panda cub is about four weeks old.

Panda cubs start following their mother when they are three months old.

A cub starts to eat **bamboo** when it is four months old. It stays with its mother for two years. After that, the panda will live alone.

Natural dangers

Adult giant pandas are not in danger from other animals. They are too big and strong to be attacked. Snow leopards sometimes catch panda **cubs**.

Snow leopards eat giant panda cubs if they can catch them.

If the weather is too cold, or the plants get a disease, the **bamboo** dies. When this happens, giant pandas can die because they have no food.

If there is no bamboo, giant pandas have nothing to eat.

Hunting and trapping

In the past, people trapped and killed giant pandas for their fur and meat. Now it is against the law to kill pandas, but some hunters still do.

This policeman has taken a panda skin away from a hunter.

This man has found a trap that is used to catch giant pandas.

Some pandas are hurt by accident. Hunters put down traps to catch other animals, such as deer. Giant pandas get badly injured if they step on the traps.

Dangers to the giant panda's world

Trees in China's mountain forests are being cut down. People are selling the wood and building towns on the land.

Destroying the forests means less food and less space for pandas.

Once a year, **male** pandas search for a **female** to **mate** with. If there are towns in the way, pandas cannot find each other easily. Fewer **cubs** are born.

These people are helping a giant panda in a tree.

How many giant pandas are there?

There are about 1,600 giant pandas in the wild today. They all live alone. Most live in small areas with fewer than 20 other pandas living nearby.

Year

1980s

2004

The number of pandas is slowly growing, but there are still not many of them.

 = 500

There are more people in China today than ever before. They use more wood and take more land to live on.

We need to protect the giant pandas' **habitat** to save them.

How are giant pandas being saved?

China has made more than 50 **reserves** for giant pandas. Reserves are areas of land where wild animals such as giant pandas can live in safety.

In reserves, people are not allowed to cut down trees.

Some reserves have **breeding centres** like this one.

In China it is against the law to hunt giant pandas. People called **wardens** protect the giant pandas in their reserve and keep hunters out.

Who is helping giant pandas?

WWF is a **charity**. It is showing people in China how to raise money to protect pandas. Today, tourists pay to watch the pandas.

The giant panda is the symbol of WWF.

Wardens *look carefully to find out where giant pandas live.*

In the Qinling (you say "Chinling") Mountains, there are 12 new panda **reserves**. The pandas can move safely from one reserve to another.

How can you help?

It is important to know that giant pandas are in danger. Then you can learn how to help to save them. Read, watch, and find out all you can about giant pandas.

*It is important to learn how to help save pandas, so that they will not become **extinct**.*

Here are some things you can do
to help.

- Join a group such as **WWF** that raises
  money for giant panda projects.
- Visit zoos where giant pandas live.
  Some zoos raise money to help wild
  giant pandas.

The future for giant pandas

Giant pandas may soon become **extinct**. In China, about half of all pandas live in **reserves**. More pandas will be saved if their **habitat** is protected.

Giant pandas could become extinct if we do not protect their habitat.

Giant pandas are having **cubs** in safe **breeding centres** in China. Some of these pandas will be set free, into the wild. Then there will be more pandas.

Breeding centres give pandas a safe place to have their babies.

Giant panda facts

- Giant pandas live for about 25 years in the wild.
- A new-born panda **cub** is only as long as a pencil.
- When giant panda cubs are born, they are pink and have no hair.
- Giant pandas are good climbers. They are also good swimmers.

More books to read

Giant Panda, Anna Claybourne (Heinemann, 2005)

Giant Panda, Edana Eckart (Children's Press, 2003)

Panda in the Park, Lucy Daniels (Hodder Children's Books, 2004)

Websites

To find out more about **WWF**, visit their website: www.wwf.org

Glossary

bamboo   a tall plant with green leaves. Pandas eat only bamboo.

breeding centre   safe place where male and female animals can mate and have babies

charity   group that collects money to help animals or people in need

cub   baby panda

extinct   when all the animals in a species die out and the species no longer exists

female   animal that can become a mother when it grows up. Women and girls are female people.

habitat   place where plants and animals grow and live. A forest is a kind of habitat.

mammal   animal that feeds its babies with the mother's milk and has some hair on its body

male   animal that can become a father when it grows up. Men and boys are male people.

mate   what male and female animals do to make babies

reserve   area of land where animals are protected and the habitat is looked after

shoot   beginning of a new plant

species   group of animals that look similar and can have babies together

warden   person who guards reserves

WWF   charity that used to be called the World Wildlife Fund

Index

bamboo 10–11, 13, 15, 31
breeding centres 23, 29, 31

China 8, 21, 22–23
claws 7
cubs 12–13, 14, 19, 29,
    30, 31

dangers 14–19

extinction 4–5, 28, 31

food 10–11, 13, 15, 30
forest cutting 18, 21
fur 6, 16

habitat 21, 28, 31
hunting 16–17

mountains 9, 25

numbers 20

paws 7, 10–11

reserves 22, 25, 28, 31

skins 16
snow leopards 14
species 4, 31

traps 16–17
tree cutting 18, 21

wardens 23, 25, 31
WWF 24, 27, 31

young pandas 12–13, 14,
    19, 29, 30

zoos 27

Titles in the *Save Our Animals!* series include:

Hardback
ISBN 10: 0 431 11421 8
ISBN 13: 978 0 431 11421 7

Hardback
ISBN 10: 0 431 11422 6
ISBN 13: 978 0 431 11422 4

Hardback
ISBN 10: 0 431 11423 4
ISBN 13: 978 0 431 11423 1

Hardback
ISBN 10: 0 431 11424 2
ISBN 13: 978 0 431 11424 8

Hardback
ISBN 10: 0 431 11425 0
ISBN 13: 978 0 431 11425 5

Hardback
ISBN 10: 0 431 11426 9
ISBN 13: 978 0 431 11426 2

Hardback
ISBN 10: 0 431 11427 7
ISBN 13: 978 0 431 11427 9

Find out about other titles from Heinemann Library on our website www.heinemann.co.uk/library